CAREERS IN
INFRASTRUCTURE BUILDING

ENGINEERS, ARCHITECTS, BUILDERS

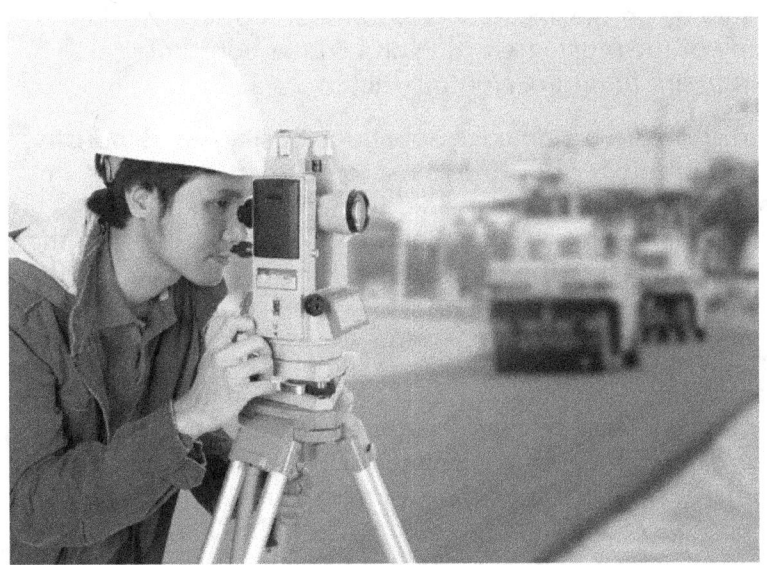

SO IT IS TIME TO CHOOSE A CAREER! This time has been coming all your life and it will have a significant effect on everything that comes after. You owe it to yourself to give this decision all the thought and study that it deserves. So think big!

Infrastructure is definitely big! Roads, bridges, dams and other public-works projects can be huge – the biggest things most people encounter on a regular basis. Infrastructure is also one of those things that people sometimes look right past, like it is not even there. Roads and bridges that people use every day exist mostly in the background. Most people do not give them much thought until they break down or fail to keep up with the times.

Building and maintaining public infrastructure are the primary function of most units of government. Your city, even if it is a small one, probably spends millions of dollars a year on infrastructure. Your state may spend billions. The federal government spends hundreds of billions of dollars each year to build and maintain its own infrastructure and provide grants to cities, counties and states. With that kind of money on the line, it should come as no surprise that some of the most interesting and contentious political battles are fought over infrastructure.

Infrastructure building is also a huge business and industry. Whether public or private, most infrastructure projects are the result of high-intensity bidding among a few well-qualified contractors. Politics always plays a role in the process, whether the contract is for the public sector or the private sector.

Infrastructure building offers a very wide range of career opportunities, from entry-level construction jobs to more professional careers in civil engineering, architecture, hydrology, and even nuclear engineering. There are also numerous opportunities in supporting career fields like finance, accounting, and management. While the word "infrastructure" has been applied to a wide variety of specialties in recent years, including information technology and even financial services, this report will focus on the more conventional types of infrastructure often known as "public works"– basically anything involving tons of concrete and steel.

WHAT YOU CAN DO NOW

THERE ARE MANY WAYS TO GET A HEAD START on your career in infrastructure building. Make an in-depth study of the infrastructure around you. Most people take infrastructure for granted. People living in modern America gripe endlessly about their daily commute without even considering how much worse it would be if not for the incredibly expensive infrastructure that allows them to get to work in the first place. The "spaghetti bowls" that typify today's highway interchanges were the stuff of science fiction only a few decades ago. Most of the superhighways, bridges, dams and other pieces of modern infrastructure that we take for granted were built since World War II. Go out and take a hard look around your world. How does your street, for example, find its way to the nearest federal highway? Where does your electricity come from? Where does the sewage go when you flush your toilet? Are the waterways where you live dammed, rerouted or embanked? If these investigations fascinate you, an infrastructure career may be a good choice for you to pursue.

Just as most people take infrastructure for granted, most people generally ignore the political process behind it. To be sure, city council debates about spending lots of money on necessities like streets and sidewalks lack the drama and urgency of negotiations over police and fire contracts, but infrastructure construction and maintenance is typically one of the largest items in a city budget. Infrastructure is where cities and their residents literally and metaphorically meet. Nobody can hold a protest on the courthouse steps until somebody builds a courthouse, so go to a few local government meetings. City councils, village boards and county boards deal constantly with infrastructure issues. Check online to get agendas in advance. Some jurisdictions also publish supporting documents like bids and ordinances online to make it easier for their residents to keep track of what is being done with their tax dollars.

You are probably not going to get hands-on experience working at a construction site. Even entry-level construction jobs have multiple requirements, the first of which is to be at least 18 years of age. You may also have to have completed an apprenticeship, belong to a union and possess very specific skills that you will need to train for. This does not mean, however, that you cannot start learning some of the skills associated with infrastructure building. Take a few shop classes while you are still in high school. Classes in mathematics, business and government will also be useful.

THE ORIGINS AND HISTORY OF INFRASTRUCTURE

INFRASTRUCTURE HAS BEEN AROUND for a long time. The word itself is a combination of the Latin prefix "infra," which means "below," and the word "structure," which is the same in English and French and describes the arrangement of and relations among the parts of something complex. The word's meaning has broadened considerably in recent decades, with just about anything that provides the basis for something else being referred to as infrastructure. The word is arguably used more commonly today within the information technology field than in the realm of public works. Cables, servers and routers make information networks possible, just like roads, bridges and tunnels make transportation networks possible. More than anything, infrastructure is a concept.

The public works infrastructure discussed in this report takes a wide variety of forms. The National Research Council – the research arm of the National Academies of Sciences, Engineering and Medicine – in 1987 drafted a comprehensive definition of public works infrastructure that refers to:

"Specific functional modes – highways, streets, roads, and bridges; mass transit; airports and airways; water supply and water resources; wastewater management; solid-waste treatment and disposal; electric power generation and transmission; telecommunications; and hazardous waste management – and the combined system these modal elements comprise. A comprehension of infrastructure spans not only these public works facilities, but also the operating procedures, management practices, and development policies that interact together with societal demand and the physical world to facilitate the transport of people and goods, provision of water for drinking and a variety of other uses, safe disposal of society's waste products, provision of energy where it is needed, and transmission of information within and between communities."

This definition from Infrastructure for the 21st Century nicely sums up the broad scope of public works infrastructure. Physical infrastructure is sometimes referred to as "hard infrastructure" while the institutions that build and maintain it are known as "soft infrastructure."

Until about 10,000 years ago there were no public works beyond, perhaps, common fire pits used by early humans to cook and provide illumination. Infrastructure is the result of the discovery of agriculture, which allowed humans to stop hunting and gathering, and settle down in one place. This is a critical juncture in human history and led to the creation of the jurisdictions we now take for granted, like cities, states and countries.

The earliest infrastructure was not planned, but created organically over time by people who needed it. Roads and trails, for example, were worn into the ground by people who naturally found the most convenient ways to get from place to place. When many people settled in the same place it became necessary to exert some control over these assets so they could be used by everybody.

Early governments were mostly local and were concerned primarily with things like maintaining a few roads around the village and keeping the well free of contamination. Roads and fresh water benefitted everybody but did not belong to anybody in particular. Governments were created in large part to manage public infrastructure on behalf of their citizens. Citizens paid regular fees to the government, which in turn used those revenues to provide infrastructure and other services that helped citizens to live better lives. This is still the way government works today. Citizens pay taxes and governments use their money to provide infrastructure and services.

This arrangement has evolved considerably over the millennia. Early infrastructure was often built by citizens themselves. People cleared trees for roads, dug wells, built fortifications and made other improvements that benefitted their villages. The Amish people of the northeastern United States still build much of their infrastructure this way, mobilizing entire villages to build barns and community centers, for example.

As governments grew and became more powerful, the job of planning was taken over by professionals. The ancient cities of Egypt, for example, were laid out with straight roads and town squares that did not happen by accident. The ancient Romans built aqueducts that can still be seen today, stretching sometimes for hundreds of miles, from water sources to the cities and towns where water was needed. Water from aqueducts irrigated farms that provided food. Roads allowed food to be taken to markets as soon as it was harvested. Public squares provided space to host the markets. Markets made money and generated additional tax revenue to build and maintain more infrastructure. Public works infrastructure helped all people to lead healthier, more prosperous lives.

Ideas about what constitutes public infrastructure have changed over time. The pyramids of Egypt, for example, were public works projects built to honor kings when they died. That may sound strange today, but modern societies still spend public money on monuments and public art that arguably qualify as infrastructure. By itself, the Washington

Monument in Washington, DC does not really do anything practical. In conjunction with other monuments, however, it does create an atmosphere that reminds residents and visitors alike that they are in the nation's capital and encourages them to think about the people and deeds to which those monuments are dedicated. For a proud national capital, this is a valuable public benefit, indeed.

Not all infrastructure is publicly owned. Many airports, for example, are owned by private corporations or by quasi-public entities nominally owned by governments but administered by private corporations. Public-private partnerships between business and government are quite common. Railroads, for example, are privately owned but could not exist without government making it possible to acquire tracts of land 50 feet wide and thousands of miles long. Power plants tend to be privately owned but are heavily regulated and require cooperation from government to do things like run power lines. Many private businesses need infrastructure of their own. Large resorts build their own marinas for watercraft, for example, and may even have their own power plants and water treatment facilities.

Whether public or private, most public works infrastructure is built by private companies that bid for contracts. Generally, a government or business identifies a need for a particular piece of infrastructure, publishes plans of where it should go and what it should do, and then advertises opportunities to bid on the project. Major projects can comprise hundreds or even thousands of individual contracts for specific items. Companies draw up proposals for the contracts they think they can win, offer to do the work for a specific price and then wait to see if they win the contract. Politics are unavoidable. Well-connected contractors often have an advantage over newcomers because they know their way around the system, which can be very complex.

Every time you flip a light switch, fill a glass with water or drive on a road you are using public works infrastructure.

WHERE YOU MAY WORK

INFRASTRUCTURE IS EVERYWHERE. Roads and bridges link us together. So do sidewalks and bike paths. Ports and airports bring commerce from around the world. Military installations host very interesting and specialized infrastructure. You can enter this field from pretty much anywhere.

How you go about it is up to you. If your goal is an entry-level construction job, you should be able to make a go of it in any sizeable metropolitan area. After you have some experience you should be able to move up in the world wherever you want. If you want to pursue a career in something like architecture or civil engineering you may have to go to where the demand is greatest. Most of the professional jobs are in major metropolitan areas even if the projects they deal with are far away. Companies that build and maintain highways, for example, do not maintain offices in the middle of nowhere even if they have contracts to pave roads there. They hire crews to do the job after the big decisions have been made around the conference table in an urban center.

Even though you can start your career just about anywhere, where you go later in life will be dictated largely by what you want to achieve. If your goal is to work on big-city infrastructure like subway systems or highways that snake through heavily developed areas without disrupting them, you need to set your sights on a career in a big city. Alternatively, if you prefer the challenge of building things like aqueducts or hazardous-waste disposal sites you should look to the countryside.

Careers in infrastructure building can also offer opportunities for adventure. American companies are in high demand around the world to design and build infrastructure beyond the capabilities of local contractors.

American contractors often compete directly for contracts with foreign governments. They also work on foreign projects for the United States government, usually through the State Department or Department of Defense. If you learn an advanced skill for which there is high demand, you should be able to build an overseas adventure or two into your career.

DESCRIPTION OF THE WORK

Civil Engineers

Civil engineering is a very diverse engineering discipline, providing the foundations for other engineering disciplines and working closely with architects and city and regional planners through every stage of the infrastructure building process. Civil engineers take the lead in designing and building roads, tunnels, dams, bridges, airports, water supply and treatment facilities, piers and wharves, drainage systems and anything else that supports the basic functions of a modern society.

Civil engineers have a wide range of responsibilities. The design work is basic, but they also have to take into account costs, regulations and legal requirements, permits, the availability of materials and the suitability of sites. Civil engineers also maintain and inspect existing infrastructure to make sure it is operating as it should.

A bachelor's degree is mandatory for this career and a master's degree is required if you want to move into senior positions. Most states require civil engineers to be licensed, and requirements vary from state to state. The American Society of Civil Engineers also offers professional certification in several areas, including water resources engineering, coastal engineering, geotechnical engineering and ports engineering, among others. Civil engineers may start out as generalists but most become specialists as they take advantage of career opportunities and learn more about what they enjoy.

Architects

Architects design buildings and other structures. While residential architects are most common, architects can specialize in infrastructure projects. In simplest terms, architects design the buildings that are associated with infrastructure. A large industrial complex, for example, may include roads, earthworks and other features that are clearly the province of civil engineers. Architects design the buildings within the complex.

There is always a little overlap between architecture and civil engineering. Civil engineers are responsible for designing and building the foundations and environs that will host the buildings designed by architects. This situation is greatly magnified in infrastructure projects, with architects and civil engineers staying in constant contact to refine their designs and make sure that everything works together as it should. Both civil engineers and architects work closely with construction managers, the professionals who manage the day-to-day activities on construction sites.

Most states require architects to possess a Bachelor of Architecture degree in order to become a licensed architect, and all states require architects to pass an examination in order to become licensed. Many architects go on to earn master's degrees in architecture both to enhance their credentials and to specialize.

Environmental Engineers

Environmental engineers are an important part of the infrastructure building process. Environmental engineers take the lead on projects of their own and play a role in projects not directly associated with environmental issues.

Environmental engineers take the lead in designing and building infrastructure that deals directly with the environment, including wastewater treatment systems and air pollution control systems. Environmental regulations are very specific for these systems, requiring specialists to handle their design and construction.

Environmental engineers also play an important role in infrastructure not directly related to the environment. All major construction projects are required to perform an environmental impact study, or EIS, before they can break ground. An EIS typically determines what the project's environmental impact will be on the water, air, land and wildlife in the vicinity of the project. Entire projects have been redesigned or even cancelled because environmental engineers determined that they would have an adverse impact on their surrounding environment. Once infrastructure has been constructed, it is the responsibility of environmental engineers to periodically assess its environmental impact and to make sure that routine maintenance is being conducted according to plan. They also take the lead in remediation projects when things go awry.

Environmental engineers work alongside architects, urban and regional planners, and civil engineers. They typically earn undergraduate degrees in environmental engineering and then go on to earn graduate degrees in an environmental specialty, like air or water pollution.

City and Regional Planners

City and regional planners are the professionals who figure out what infrastructure is needed and where it should go. Planners work either for city, county, state or federal government agencies, or for private contracting companies. A bachelor's degree is required to enter this profession and a master's degree is highly recommended.

The scope of a planner's responsibilities depends largely upon the planner's employer. Even city planners for relatively small cities have a role to play in building and maintaining infrastructure. City planners decide where things should be built, like roads, bridges, and parking lots. City planners also take the lead in devising zoning districts for their cities. Zoning determines what land can be used for in specific areas: residential districts are for homes, commercial districts are for retail businesses, and industrial districts are for heavier industry. Each district requires its own kind of infrastructure.

Regional planners do essentially the same thing but on a larger scale. Where city planners are concerned with streets, regional planners are more concerned about highways. Regional planners are also responsible for determining the need for bridges, tunnels, waterworks, wastewater treatment facilities, airports and railroad right-of-ways. City planners may participate in some of these tasks, especially if they work in a big city, but regional planners are responsible for figuring out the infrastructure that ties cities together.

Planners are not engineers. They do not design bridges, for example. They do, however, look at factors like population growth, commuting patterns and opportunities for economic development to determine where bridges are needed. They perform the same process for other types of infrastructure. After they have identified a need, the process moves along to the engineers and architects who will bring the infrastructure to life.

Elected Officials

Elected officials control the purse strings. They write the laws that collect the taxes and then decide what to do with the tax revenue. Ideally, they do this in conjunction with the needs of their constituents. If the citizens of their jurisdiction need a new sewage treatment plant, for example, they work hard to get enough votes in the legislature to get one built. Along the way they make compromises with other elected officials and with specific constituencies who have a special interest in the project. People who live near the site proposed for a sewage treatment plant may want to make sure that any effluent – steam from the treatment process – is filtered to remove noxious smells. Environmentalists may insist that the plant use the very latest technology to get water as clean as possible. There could be many other issues, depending upon the nature of the project.

If you want to get to the heart of the infrastructure building process, make it a goal to get yourself elected to a position in a legislature. This is not as daunting as it sounds. Most local elected officials serving in city councils and county boards are part-timers who have regular jobs most of the time. You do not have to make politics your full-time career, but serving a term or two will open your eyes in many ways.

STORIES OF INFRASTRUCTURE PROFESSIONALS

I Am a Commercial Architect

"As an architect it would be easy for me to say simply that I design buildings. That's true, but I also design related structures and work closely with civil engineers to create complete spaces filled with buildings and connective structures like roads, walkways, bridges and whatever else may be needed. To me, architecture is art – art with a purpose.

I doodled a lot as a kid. When my friends were drawing simple houses with four windows and a door dead center I was dreaming up skyscrapers and houses with walls built at crazy angles. I was fascinated by the possibilities presented by architecture and wanted to spend my life learning all I could.

I majored in architecture in college, of course, and went on to earn a master's degree in architecture, known as a M.Arch degree, and then to become certified in my state. Licensure is very important for architects. Nobody wants to live or work in a building that has been designed by an amateur. That would be dangerous.

I currently work for an enormous company that usually serves as the prime contractor for very large projects. As the prime contractor, it is up to us to hire smaller companies, known as subcontractors, to make sure we have all the expertise we need to get the job done. We have taken the lead on all sorts of projects, from airports to industrial parks to commercial ports. We are a very, very large company and routinely work on projects for the federal government and very large corporations.

As an architect, it is my job to design buildings and other structures that are required by the infrastructure project. This can include fairly conventional office buildings, and utterly unconventional buildings like hangars for unusual aircraft, and just about anything else you can dream up. I have to work very closely with civil engineers to make sure that my creations and theirs work together. My buildings wouldn't be worth much without their infrastructure and their infrastructure wouldn't have a purpose without my buildings. We generally come up with our initial plans separately and then get together and thrash out our differences until we have a complete plan that works for everybody. The collaborative process can be trying, but it can also be fun. Your work may be spectacular, but it has to fit into a larger plan."

I Am a Civil Engineer

"I have always thought of civil engineering as the engineering discipline that brings all of the other engineering disciplines together. Electrical engineers design generators, for example, and mechanical engineers design mechanical systems but those generators and systems can't do much until they are installed in suitable infrastructure. That's where civil engineers come in. We build the structures that support everything else.

I got into this profession because I have always been fascinated by public works infrastructure. Have you ever given serious thought to how the street in front of your house got there, and how it connects you to the rest of the world? Or what happens when you flush your toilet or flip a light switch? I have, and it's all fascinating.

I started my career as a builder in the Navy. Builders, known by our rating abbreviation as BUs, make up the largest contingent of the famous Navy Seabees, the Navy's in-house civil engineering and construction battalion. I joined the Navy after high school and immediately entered the builder specialty. Boot camp and builder training took about nine months and then I was shipped off to my first command. For the next five years I helped to build everything from piers and wharves to fitness centers and runways, and I did my job all over the world. I learned a lot in those five years, and wouldn't trade them for anything. They gave me an excellent foundation in the basics of civil engineering and made me eligible for the GI Bill, which I used to earn a bachelor's degree in civil engineering after I left active duty. I stayed in the Navy Reserve after leaving active duty and am now a part-time officer in the Seabees.

After earning my bachelor 's degree, I got a job with the contracting company where I completed an internship, which is very common. This company specialized in all things concrete, and the bigger, the better. We poured concrete for huge projects like sewage treatment plants, tunnels and highways. We worked in conjunction with other contractors to design and build infrastructure, mostly for local and state governments. I also earned a master's degree in civil engineering by going to school part time.

Nowadays I work for a company that specializes in building infrastructure in what are called "austere environments." Environments where you might have to live in a tent, eat all of your meals out of a can and have no creature comforts. Places like Afghanistan and Uganda, to name a few. My company specializes in building small airports in out-of-the-way places. We often work alongside Navy Seabees and their compatriots from the other services. I can't get into too many details, but let's just say that the work can be very exciting.

I'd recommend this career to anybody who has the

aptitude and likes to dream big. Civil engineers make everything else come together. Architects may get to design the beautiful buildings that everybody can see but they wouldn't get very far without civil engineers to build their foundations."

I Am a Regional Planner

"I am a regional planner for a large Midwestern state. I work in the northern part of the state, where most of the people are, and serve alongside planners from cities and counties. As a state-level planner, my job is often to figure out how to bring city and county planners together and agree on a way forward.

Most infrastructure is funded by a combination of local, state and federal money. That gives planners and elected officials from several different governments a say in most infrastructure projects. Sorting out everybody's differences is the name of the game. A highway interchange, for example, may be funded mostly by federal money but constructed under the auspices of a state highway department with input from cities and counties whose residents and businesses will use the interchange the most.

As a state level planner, when I work on a highway project I am mostly concerned with the big picture of how people and commerce move around the state as a whole. This is easy when the subject is a stretch of highway through farmland in the middle of the state. It gets a lot harder when the project is an interchange in a populated area bounded by several cities and parcels of unincorporated county. The city planners are more concerned about the details of the project. Will the interchange have an adverse impact on homes and business already in the area? Will moving the project a mile or so solve problems or create them? What new economic opportunities may be presented by the increased traffic flow offered by the interchange? Sorting it all out can be frustrating and fun at the same time.

I also work alongside civil engineers and architects to make sure that their designs will meet the needs I have identified. If my calculations say that the new interchange needs to handle five times as many vehicles as the current arrangement then that's what the civil engineers have to shoot for. If they come up with a design that can only handle four times as much traffic, they will have to go back to the drawing board. They may have a good reason that will force me to change my assumptions. If they come up with a design that can handle six times the current traffic and do it for the same price as the original proposal that will make everyone happy.

I earned a bachelor's degree in regional planning after high school and completed an internship with a medium-sized city. I quickly discovered that planning isn't all about creating the perfect utopia for everybody. It's about doing the best you can within the constraints of money and politics. Compromise is the name of the game."

I Own a Contracting Company

"I own a medium-sized contracting company. We specialize in basic infrastructure like roadbeds and building foundations, but we can also do marine infrastructure like embankments and piers.

I started out as a civil engineer. I majored in civil engineering in college and worked my way up through the ranks at several companies before deciding to start my own. As in most businesses, your duties tend to become more about management and leadership as you move up the ladder in the civil engineering business. In my case, I don't really do hands-on civil engineering any more. I hire other people to do that because I have to run the business.

I typically take the lead in preparing bids and conducting negotiations to compete for contracts. I spend much of my time picking through the websites of cities and states in my part of the country to stay on top of new requests for proposals, or RFPs. An RFP is what a government agency or business puts out when they need something.

I recently came across an RFP for a recreational marina advertised by a small city on the shore of a large lake. The city wanted 300 slips, piers, embankments, a clubhouse, maintenance sheds, cranes and other facilities commonly associated with a marina. My company has done plenty of waterway business in the past, I put together a proposal and sent it in. I'm very happy to say that we won the business.

Winning a contract is no mean feat. Generally speaking, you have to promise to deliver everything in the RFP and to do so for less money than any of your competitors. Government agencies have an obligation to use their taxpayers' money wisely, so the lowest bidder almost always gets the job. Winning also involves going to a lot of city council meetings, buying a lot of lunches, and generally keeping my head in the game at all times.

After a contract has been won, it is my job to figure out how to fulfill it. This usually involves hiring subcontractors to take on specific parts of the project. For very large projects I may issue my own RFPs to get help for the parts of the project that I can't do with my in-house resources. Very few contracting companies own and operate all of the assets they need to build infrastructure. The nature of the business makes this impossible. I don't own 100 dump trucks, for example, because I would have no use for them in-between jobs. I only employ about 75 people full time but may employ thousands for a few months or years for a large project. The additional people work for the subcontractors I hire. When the contract has been fulfilled, those companies move on.

I enjoy this business because I have never gotten over my fascination with infrastructure. The things we take for granted today, the things we use every day, would be mind boggling to our grandparents. Infrastructure expands opportunity for everybody and makes the world a better place."

PERSONAL QUALIFICATIONS

INFRASTRUCTURE BUILDING OFFERS many career paths but there are some personal qualities you should possess if you want to make the most of your career. You should be able to take a comprehensive view of challenges and be able to break them down into manageable parts. Whether you are the chief executive officer of the company building the project or one of the many workers toiling at the construction site, you should be able to see the big picture at all times. Some infrastructure projects, like roads and bridges, have very clear functions that are easy to visualize. Other types of infrastructure, like a hazardous waste containment facility, may look like little more than holes in the ground. Infrastructure professionals have to be able to keep the goal in mind at all times even while working on small steps along the way. Professionals call this "working backwards." First, a need has to be identified. A state legislator, for example, may say that there is a need for a highway interchange in a part of the state that has seen rapid growth in recent years. Experts conduct a study and determine that a high-capacity interchange would alleviate congestion in the area. So what will it take to make a new interchange a reality? This is when professionals start to work backwards. Architects and civil engineers draft basic conceptions of what the interchange should look like, and then a small army of experts dissect the finished product and determine all the steps needed to make it a reality. Each step becomes a relatively simple part of the much larger and more complex project. Each step can also become a separate contract for work on that piece.

The best infrastructure professionals stay on top of advances in their fields. Doing so not only helps them to deliver the best possible product, it also helps them to more quickly dismiss bad ideas or ideas that are simply out-of-date. Nobody would use stone to build a bridge in this day and age, unless that bridge was very small and mostly for ornamental purposes. Steel-reinforced concrete works much better, allowing for greater spans and heavier loads. Civil engineers and architects constantly devise new ways to do things, and those ways are generally better and less expensive than the old ways they replace.

You have undoubtedly been told that patience is a virtue. It is doubly true for professionals in the infrastructure business. Major projects routinely go over budget and past their scheduled completion date. An oft-cited example of this tendency is the rerouting of Interstate 93 through the center of Boston, commonly known as the "Big Dig." Begun in 1982 with a scheduled completion date of 1998 – already a long time – the project was not completed until 2007. The original budget also ballooned from $2.8 billion to $14.6 billion. The project was so badly executed that many of the contractors involved had to pay fines and one worker died in a construction accident. The planning of Millennium Park in Chicago – so named because it was anticipated to be finished to celebrate the new millennium – began in 1997. Construction began in 1998, and Millennium Park was opened in 2004, four years behind schedule. Even the best-executed infrastructure projects can take years to complete, and rarely does everything go exactly as planned.

ATTRACTIVE FEATURES

THERE IS MUCH TO LIKE ABOUT A CAREER in infrastructure building. You can play an important role in the American adventure. Hoover Dam, near Las Vegas, Nevada, is the stuff of legend. Begun in 1931 and completed in 1936, Hoover Dam was the largest concrete structure in the world at the time of its construction. It was built by a private consortium – a group of companies – called Six Companies, Inc. under contract to the federal government and employed thousands of workers during the Great Depression, a period of great economic instability. More than 100 people died during its construction. The concrete at its base is so thick that engineers believe that it has not completely set, even more than 80 years after its construction. It is an amazing feat of engineering and sheer human determination. The dam's generators provide electricity to Nevada, Arizona and California. While most infrastructure is largely ignored, the Hoover Dam's sheer awesomeness attracts more than a million tourists per year. If you ever find yourself in Las Vegas, you owe it to yourself to get out of town and see it up close. The Hoover Dam is a textbook example of how exciting infrastructure can be, and the people who built it had every right to take pride in their contribution, whether they designed the generators or simply turned a shovel.

Not everybody has the opportunity to participate in such a grand project. If you pursue a career in infrastructure building, however, grand projects could become your daily life.

It takes many people and many different skills to build something as large and complicated as the Hoover Dam or a complex highway interchange. As such, you can enter this business from any number of angles. You could start your career as a construction worker, maybe put- ting in part-time hours while you go to college to earn a degree in civil engineering. Later in your career you could become a senior executive with a contracting company. Given all the connections you would make over a few decades in the business, it would seem natural for you to get into politics later in life and help to make the big decisions from the other side of the desk.

Job security is very good. Politics and economic downturns can sometimes delay the construction of new infrastructure, but existing infrastructure always needs maintenance. That is why major contracting companies generally possess the ability to both build new infrastructure and maintain it after it is finished. The demand for infrastructure never goes down. Roads and bridges almost never go away after they have been built, and as long as the population continues to grow there will always be demand for new infrastructure.

UNATTRACTIVE ASPECTS

THE INFRASTRUCTURE BUSINESS IS A VERY difficult business. Politics infect every decision. The overwhelming majority of infrastructure projects are funded by the public sector. They are government projects paid for with taxpayer dollars doled out through the political process. This means that getting major infrastructure projects off the ground can take a very long time and can be delayed or even derailed by a wide variety of unexpected twists and turns. The rise of environmental awareness, for example, has led to new requirements for infrastructure projects that never would have been considered when the Hoover Dam was built. What is the potential effect upon the fish that live in the waterway to be dammed? How many trees will be cut down? How much dust will be generated by the construction process? How many decibels of noise? Are enough of the contracting companies owned by women or minorities? Will the project create many jobs for people who live in the area? All of these issues must be tackled before a major project can get the green light to move forward.

The California High-Speed Rail Authority was founded in 1996 to build a high-speed railway connecting San Francisco and Los Angeles. The authority broke ground in 2015, 19 years after its founding, and is predicting that the first passengers will be able to ride a small portion of the route by sometime between 2025 and 2029. That is about 30 years from creating a government agency to actually providing a service, and that is not counting the years of negotiation that went into creating the agency in the first place. Many California citizens have concluded that does not make sense, and they may hold the politicians and infrastructure professionals accountable.

Infrastructure does not come cheap. The final cost of the California high-speed railway is currently predicted to be about $65 billion. That is almost twice as much as the $33 billion figure originally approved by California voters in 2008. Cost overruns like these have to do with politics, but they also underscore the fundamental nature of infrastructure – it is expensive. Contracting companies who want to be competitive for infrastructure projects have to make enormous investments in capital equipment like cranes and heavy-duty vehicles, and in highly paid professionals like architects and civil engineers. Even for a relatively small contractor going after a tiny subcontract, is can cost millions to get started.

Entrepreneurship is not impossible in this business but it is not easy. A small company can bid on a piece of electrical or plumbing work. The subcontractors who do the small jobs may do very well, and starting out as a subcontractor is an excellent way to get into the business. Prime contractors are multibillion-dollar companies with sizeable capitalization and a very wide range of capabilities at their disposal.

EDUCATION AND TRAINING

EXACTLY WHAT KIND OF EDUCATION AND TRAINING you will need for your career depends upon the route you want to take. Some professions, like civil engineering or architecture, and specialties like hydrology or nuclear engineering, will require you to head straight to college, and also spend a few additional years earning a master's degree.

If you have set your sights on one of the building trades, like plumbing or electrical work, you should look into an apprenticeship.

Careerists on track to enter an infrastructure profession should start preparing in high school. You will need excellent grades in order to get into competitive programs in engineering, architecture or similar professions. You will also need the knowledge and prerequisites.

You may have your heart set on a specific career path right now. You should know, however, that most college students change their majors once or twice as they discover new preferences and opportunities. Given the incredibly broad array of opportunities within the infrastructure business, you could eventually change your major from architecture to engineering to business.

The path to a profession in the infrastructure business may require a graduate degree at some point, and certainly if you want to get ahead in the world. Engineers with master's degrees are very common, as are business leaders with Master of Business Administration degrees (MBAs).

If you take the college route be sure to take advantage of the opportunity to complete an internship. Interns work alongside professionals to get an inside view of the career they think they want to pursue. It is very common for college graduates to get their first job with the company they interned with.

Most careers in the building trades begin with an apprenticeship. Often associated with a union or a community college, most apprenticeships spell out a training program of three to five years, consisting of classroom study combined with hands-on experience under the supervision of an experienced professional. Apprenticeship requirements vary widely from one state to the next, so look into the opportunities that may be available where you live. Apprenticeships also vary depending on the particular trade.

Service in the United States military is an excellent way to get started. The military maintains a network of hundreds of bases all over the world, all of which involve extensive infrastructure. Runways, bunkers, depots, and piers are just some of the types of infrastructure maintained by the military. Military infrastructure is built and maintained by a combination of military personnel, government employed civilians, and contractors from the private sector. You could find yourself working in military infrastructure even if you never spend a day in uniform. All of the services offer training in jobs related to the infrastructure business. The Navy, for example, deploys Naval Construction Battalions – known as Seabees – all over the world to build and maintain infrastructure for the US Navy, other American military forces and foreign allies and partners. A five-year hitch in the military will not only set you up with skills and experience, it will also make you eligible for the GI Bill, which can pay for college or vocational training, and the VA Loan, which will help you to buy a home. Not everybody is cut out for a 30-year career in the military but a five-year hitch early in life can set you up for success.

EARNINGS

EARNINGS VARY WIDELY IN THE INFRASTRUCTURE business, from laborers paid by the hour to senior executives at major construction companies. You will probably find yourself on many rungs of this ladder if you pursue this career, starting at the bottom, working your way up and maybe even making a few lateral moves.

Day laborers may be paid as little as the minimum wage, which currently ranges from the federal minimum of $7.25 per hour to as high as $15 per hour in some jurisdictions. Day laborers who belong to unions or possess specific skills may be paid somewhat more. Fringe benefits like paid vacation time or health insurance may or may not be offered at this level.

Full-time construction workers with experience and advanced skills can earn anywhere from $50,000 to $75,000 per year depending upon their skill, seniority and location in the country. Construction managers earn somewhat more and generally work their way up into managerial positions.

Civil engineers with a master's degree can earn anywhere from $75,000 to $125,000 per year, and maybe more if they possess very advanced skills or have a particularly impressive track record of success. Architects can earn from $75,000 to $150,000 per year, also depending upon their individual qualifications and track record. Highly specialized professionals like hydrologists and nuclear engineers can expect similar earnings.

Many of the career paths in infrastructure are in the public sector, which maintains fairly rigid salary schedules. Cities, states and the federal government all have their own pay tables, some of which are quite generous. The general pay schedule for federal employees, for example, starts at GS-1 – for General Schedule, the pay schedule for most federal employees – and tops out at GS-15. The base pay for a

GS-15 at step 10, the highest step, is currently $134,776 per year, and can be higher depending upon locality.

OPPORTUNITIES

BECAUSE INFRASTRUCTURE IS BOTH IMPORTANT and ever-present, there are always opportunities to get into the business. America's infrastructure deficit could provide incredible opportunities for the next few years. The exact assessments vary but everybody agrees that the United States has a major infrastructure problem. Our roads, bridges, waterways, railroads, airports, dams and other infrastructure are in need of repair and renovation. Although most American infrastructure is owned and operated by state and local governments, much of the money required for major projects comes from the federal government in Washington, DC. The federal government has many responsibilities and not enough money for every need, making infrastructure renovation a tough sell to members of Congress. The Trump administration has made infrastructure a top priority, however, and could succeed in funding more infrastructure improvements than any other administration in recent years. If this push comes to fruition, even if only in part, it could open up opportunities in infrastructure building for quite a long time.

Increased federal funding means more opportunities for contractors from the private sector. Private companies have always done most of infrastructure design and construction, but private companies cannot even begin to work until a government entity has identified a need and advertised a request for proposal. New infrastructure spending will lead to a flood of RFPs and new business for private contractors.

Many opportunities will be for relatively short periods of time. Most infrastructure business is characterized by a flurry of activity in the beginning, as infrastructure is designed and built, and then a long, steady period of maintenance that may be carried out by private contractors or government employees. Many companies hire infrastructure professionals for the duration of a contract, rather than as permanent employees. When you go in search of your first job be ready to jump at these short-term opportunities.

GETTING STARTED

GET YOUR PERSONAL MARKETING MATERIALS in order, especially your résumé. Take the time to do it right. If you are not confident in your own résumé writing skills there are innumerable books and software applications available to help you. Your university or apprenticeship program may also offer assistance. Make sure to write a detailed résumé including everything you have ever done. You can then use this master résumé as your source for resumes aimed at specific jobs by cutting and pasting the most important parts into a new résumé tailored to get you the job that you want.

Get in touch with people who can offer you jobs. Start with people you already know. Connections you made during your internship or apprenticeship are critical. Even if they do not have anything to offer you right away, they may be inclined to help you out by forwarding your résumé to somebody who does, or by keeping you in the back of their mind for when something opens up. You should also get your résumé onto job-search websites and into the hands of hiring personnel by responding to help-wanted listings on the web. There is no excuse for not getting your résumé into the hands of at least 100 potential employers.

As you assess the opportunities available and think about where you want to go with your career resist the urge to focus too much on landing your dream job. As a newcomer to the world of work you only think you know what your dream job would be. You will have a much better idea after you have spent a few years in the workforce. This is a good reason to delay graduate school, too. Keep an open mind and opportunities will come your way. Good luck!

ASSOCIATIONS, PERIODICALS, WEBSITES

■ **American Association of Port Authorities**
www.aapa-ports.org

■ **American Concrete Institute**
www.concrete.org

■ **American Council of Engineering Companies**
www.acec.org

■ **American Institute of Architects**
www.aia.org

■ **American Public Power Association**
www.publicpower.org

■ **American Public Works Association**
www.apwa.net

■ **American Road and Transportation Builders Association**
www.artba.org

■ **American Society for Engineering Education**
www.asee.org

■ **American Society of Metals**
www.asminternational.org

■ **American Society of Civil Engineers**
www.asce.org

■ **Bechtel Group**
www.bechtel.com

■ **Contour Global**
www.contourglobal.com

■ **Earthquake Engineers Research Institute**
www.eeri.org

■ **Electric Power Research Institute**
www.epri.com

■ **Energy Equipment and Infrastructure Alliance**
www.eeia.org

■ **Fluor**
www.fluor.com

■ **Gas Technology Institute**
www.gastechnology.org

■ **Infrastructure Report Card**
www.infrastructurereportcard.org

■ **Infrastructure Week**
www.infrastructureweek.org

■ **Institute for Sustainable Infrastructure**
www.sustainableinfrastructure.org

■ **International Society for Soil Mechanics and Geotechnical Engineering**
www.issmge.org

■ National Association of Manufacturers
www.nam.org

■ Nuclear Energy Institute
www.nei.org

■ Society of American Registered Architects
www.sara-national.org

■ Solar Energy Industries Association
www.seia.org

■ Tetra Tech
www.tetratech.com

■ United States Agency for International
Development
www.usaid.gov

■ United States Department of Transportation
www.dot.gov

■ United States Energy Association
www.usea.org

■ United States Society of Dams
www.ussdams.org
■ US Water Alliance
www.uswateralliance.org

Institute For Career Research CHICAGO

CAREERS INTERNET DATABASE
www.careers-internet.org

www.ingramcontent.com/pod-product-compliance
Lightning Source LLC
Chambersburg PA
CBHW070522220526
45467CB00002B/800